A STEP-BY-STEP TUTORIAL
FOR GETTING STARTED TODAY

TANTEK ÇELIK

HTML5 Now
A Step-by-Step Tutorial for Getting Started Today
Tantek Çelik

New Riders
1249 Eighth Street
Berkeley, CA 94710
510/524-2178
Fax: 510/524-2221
Find us on the Web at www.newriders.com

To report errors, please send a note to errata@peachpit.com
New Riders is an imprint of Peachpit, a division of Pearson Education

Senior Editor: Karyn Johnson
Production Editor: Hilal Sala
Copy Editor: Kelly Anton
Technical Editor: Ben Ward
Interior Design and Composition: Andreas deDanaan
Presentation Graphics and Design: Coley Wopperer
Author Photo: Matt Nuzzaco
Cover Design: Mimi Heft
Cover Production: Andreas deDanaan
Video Production and Direction: Mary Sweeney

ISBN-13: 978-0-321-71991-1
ISBN-10:   0-321-71991-3

9 8 7 6 5 4 3 2 1

Printed and bound in the United States of America

CONTENTS

01
INTRODUCTION

"In times of profound change, the learners inherit the earth, while the learned find them-selves beautifully equipped to deal with a world that no longer exists."

    — *Eric Hoffer*

We are in the midst of the biggest change in web development since Cascading Style Sheets (CSS) cleansed our content of presentational markup and inspired us to think outside table layout boxes.

HTML5 and related technologies are upgrading the potential of the web with

- simplification, cleanup, and fixes to HTML4 and XHTML
- richer semantic markup
- new forms capabilities
- native multimedia
- programmable vector graphics
- powerful, bleeding-edge APIs

HTML5 Now provides you with HTML5 examples, tutorials, and explanations you can use today, with details of what you can start enhancing, what to be careful with, and what you can start experimenting with to get a head start.

ON THE DVD: EXTENDED VERSION OF GUIDE

On the included DVD, you will find a 100-page extended version of this reference guide with additional examples. This PDF is searchable and contains hyperlinks, which are shown in blue text.

02
BACKGROUND: WHERE DID HTML5 COME FROM?

Tim Berners-Lee first documented, proposed, implemented, and wrote HTML in the early 1990s, and the evolution of HTML slowly accelerated for nearly a decade.

FROM EVOLUTION TO REVOLUTION AND BACK

In the trailing years of the web's first decade, the World Wide Web Consortium (W3C) pursued the revolution of XML, with its promise of bringing cleaner, limitless markup, and enabling everyone to make up their own tags for even richer expression. However, while XML did liberate many corporations from proprietary formats and protocols on their intranets, the envisioned XML-based World Wide Web never materialized.

In the early 2000s, the modern web design community adopted XHTML 1.0 in ways compatible with the existing web. Leaders in the community rallied designers and developers around their best practices of standards-based design, using CSS for presentation, and maximizing the use of semantic markup.

THE "GREAT WEB SCHISM" OF 2004

In 2004, the W3C held a two day workshop in San Jose, California on Web Applications and Compound Documents. The conclusion was nothing short of a schism between browser makers and the W3C regarding approaches to web standards. A poll taken at the end of the workshop showed that browser makers unanimously favored an incremental approach based on evolving HTML4/XHTML1 + CSS + DOM, in contrast to the more dominant position led by W3C staff (and a few minor vendors) advocating replacing that stack with non-backward-compatible XHTML2 + XForms + SVG + MathML + RDFa.

MICROFORMATS AND THE WHATWG

The concept of microformats — extending Web semantics using existing valid semantic HTML4 and XHTML1 — would leap forward just three months following that fateful workshop, with the introduction of hCalendar and hCard. It birthed a new standards community in 2005: microformats.org.

The browser makers went on to form The Web Hypertext Application Technologies Working Group (WHATWG) to pursue the evolution of HTML itself and new APIs for web applications. They published the first specifications for "Web Applications 1.0" as well as an update of "Web Forms 2.0." Meanwhile, W3C largely ignored both efforts and continued to pour time and effort into XHTML 2.0.

MICROSOFT'S NEUTRAL STANCE

Microsoft, whose delegates agreed with and voted in the poll alongside other browser makers, chose to stay neutral, agreeing in principle yet declined to join the WHATWG and simultaneously left the W3C's XHTML 2.0 effort.

Browsers began to implement portions of Web Apps 1.0 and Web Forms 2.0, which merged and were renamed to "HTML5". In 2007 the W3C started a new HTML working group to adopt and develop HTML5 in cooperation with the WHATWG. In 2009, the W3C finally closed the XHTML2 working group and stopped work on XHTML2. The world of web standards had finally begun to re-converge.

03
HTML5 OVERVIEW

Eager to get started with HTML5? In this tutorial, you'll learn

- how to create your first HTML5 page
- key transitions from HTML4/XHTML1 and validating
- new semantics and audio, video, and canvas
- new forms features
- bleeding-edge APIs for web applications

04
HTML5 BASICS

Here are some typographical conventions used in this tutorial:

CONVENTION	DESCRIPTION
`monospace`	Code in general is shown in monospace type.
`bold gray Monospace`	Old or obsolete code is bold , gray, italicized.
`bold orange monospace`	Transitional code is orange, bold, dotted-underlined.
`bold fuchsia monospace`	New and recommended code is fuchsia and bold.
blue text	hyperlinked text

NEW DOCTYPE

Currently you may be using an XHTML1 DOCTYPE like this in your web pages:

```
<!DOCTYPE html PUBLIC
 "-//W3C//DTD XHTML 1.0 Strict//EN"
 "http://www.w3.org/TR/xhtml1/DTD/xhtml1-strict.dtd">
```

HTML5 has drastically shortened the DOCTYPE:

```
<!DOCTYPE html>
```

That's it — just 15 characters. Short enough to type from memory.

SIMPLER CHARACTER SET CODE

On the web, people express themselves in numerous languages, with potentially thousands of different characters, glyphs, and symbols. In the past, web developers from different countries had to use different character sets to encode their content for the web. Unicode has solved that problem, and UTF-8 is the simplest and most backward-compatible encoding for Unicode.

Before HTML5, here's how you would do so:

```
<meta
 http-equiv="content-type" content="text/html;
     charset=utf-8">
```

HTML5 has shortened this essential meta tag down to 22 characters.

```
<meta charset="utf-8">
```

YOUR FIRST HTML5 DOCUMENT

You only need two more things to complete your first HTML5 document. First, add a `<title>` element just as you would in previous versions of HTML:

```
<title>Hello</title>
```

Second, add just a bit of content, perhaps with a paragraph tag:

```
<p>
World Wide Web
</p>
```

All put together:

```
<!DOCTYPE html>
<meta charset="utf-8">
<title>Hello</title>
<p>
World Wide Web
</p>
```

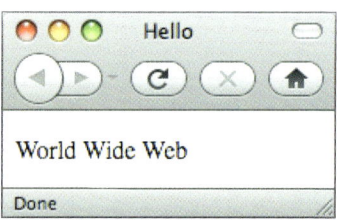

What it looks like in a browser

05
HTML5 TRANSITION

Now that you know how to create an HTML5 document from scratch, let's talk about how to transition your existing documents.

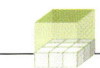

REMOVE PRESENTATIONAL MARKUP

For those of you still using "Transitional" DOCTYPES, time is up. To embrace HTML5, you must remove all presentational markup.

Here's a simple summary of what to replace:

PRESENTATIONAL MARKUP	CSS REPLACEMENT
<basefont> <big> <font> <tt>	`font` properties
<s> <strike> <u>	`text-decoration`
<center> and *align=center*	`text-align:center` and `margin:auto`
align=left, *right*, or *justify* on `<div>` and other text elements	`text-align:left`, `right`, `justify` respectively
align=left or *align=right* on `<img>` and other replaced elements	`float:left` and `float:right` respectively
<body text link alink vlink>	`color` property and `:link`, `:visited`, `:active` pseudo-classes
<body background>	`background-image`
bgcolor attribute	`background-color`
border attribute and *<table frame rules>*	`border` properties
<table cellspacing>	`border-spacing`
<table cellpadding>	`padding` on the table cells (`<th>` and `<td>`) themselves
<br clear>	`clear`
hspace, *vspace*, *marginheight*, *marginwidth*	`margin` properties
<hr noshade size>	`border-style:solid` and `border-width`
nowrap attribute	`white-space:nowrap`
valign attribute	`vertical-align`
height and *width* attributes	`height` and `width` properties
<plaintext>	No CSS for this. Use `<pre>` or serve that content as `text/plain`, not HTML

REMOVE FAILED FEATURES

HTML5 goes beyond purging presentational markup and has removed failed features as well. Thus, you must remove these tags from your HTML as well.

FAILED HTML4 FEATURE	USE THIS INSTEAD
`<img longdesc>`	use a visible description or link to one
`<frameset> <frame>`	redesign your content, with `<iframe>` if necessary
`<html version>`	nothing, just drop the version attribute.
`<meta scheme>`	avoid all invisible metadata, add microformats to visible content instead
rev attribute	use `rel` microformats instead

JUST FOR COMPATIBILITY

The *border* attribute on `<img>` is there to undo a default presentational annoyance from certain older browsers (blue border on hyperlinked images).

HTML5 permits `border="0"` (no other values) on `<img>` (no other tag):

`<a href="..."><img border="0"></a>`

I think the border attribute is unnecessary and a bit of CSS is sufficient:

`:link img,:visited img { border:0; }`

The second bit of compatibility markup has to do with scripting. In HTML5, the *type* attribute is no longer necessary on the `<script>` tag. Some older browsers may require that you specify the language explicitly. HTML5 permits type=`"text/javascript"` on the `<script>` tag:

`<script type="text/javascript">`

TRANSITIONING YOUR XHTML

HTML5 permits you to continue to maintain XHTML compatibility. A few simple rules will take care of most of the work for you and help keep your code clean and consistent.

1. SELF-CLOSE EMPTY HTML4 TAGS

A handful of elements in HTML4 never have close tags. In order for them to be properly parsed by XML processors, you need to use XML self-closing syntax.

In short, put a slash (/) just inside the closing angle bracket (>) on these tags: `<br/>`, `<hr/>`, `<img/>`, `<input/>`, `<link/>`, `<meta/>`, `<option/>`

2. ALWAYS USE QUOTED ATTRIBUTE VALUES

XHTML requires all attribute values to be quoted. Quoting attribute values is a good habit that will help you avoid inadvertent errors.

`<img src="photo1.jpg" alt="photograph"/`

3. USE EXPLICIT TAGS FOR A CONSISTENT DOM

In the previous section we constructed a simple HTML5 document:

```
<!DOCTYPE html>
<meta charset="utf-8">
<title>Hello</title>
<p>
World Wide Web
</p>
```

We noted that it lacked `<html>`, `<head>`, and `<body>` tags — because it doesn't actually need them since they're implied.

In XML (and thus XHTML), there are no implied tag; you need to write them out yourself. We're going to self-close the meta tag, too:

```
<!DOCTYPE html>
<html>
<head>
```

```
<meta charset="utf-8" />
<title>Hello</title>
</head>
<body>
<p>
World Wide Web
</p>
</body>
</html>
```

UPDATE OBSOLETE MARKUP

HTML5 has finally done away with a few more deprecated HTML4 tags and attributes that don't fall into any of the above categories. If your code uses of any of these, be sure to use the equivalent instead.

REMOVED HTML4 FEATURE	HTML5 REPLACEMENT
<acronym>	*<abbr>*
<applet>	*<object>*
<dir>	*<ul>*
<a name="a1"></a>	*<div id="a1"> ... </div>*
<img *name="i1">*	<img *id="i1"* />

06
NOTABLE CHANGES
TO HTML4 FEATURES

Several HTML4 features have been refined in HTML5, several former presentational tags received new semantic lives, and some black sheep markup has been welcomed into the fold.

SEMANTIC REFINEMENTS TO HTML4 ELEMENTS

First, let's take a look at what has been improved through refinement.

NESTABLE <EM>PHASIS ELEMENTS

HTML4 used the `<strong>` element to indicate stronger emphasis. In HTML5, instead use another `<em>` element to indicate stronger emphasis.

OLD HTML4 SEMANTIC MARKUP	NOW IN HTML5
`<strong>...</strong>`	`<em><em>...</em></em>`

`<em> ...`
`    <strong>...</strong> ...`
`</em>`
	`<em> ...`
	`    <em>...</em> ...`
	`</em>`

When you update your uses of `<strong>` to nested `<em>` elements, you'll want to rewrite your CSS, since nested `<em>` elements look no different by default.

```
em              { font-style:italic }
em em           { font-weight:bold }
```

Has `<strong>` been forgotten? Not forgotten, but repurposed.

THE IMPORTANCE OF <STRONG>

The <strong> element has been redefined to mean "importance" rather than "strong emphasis." Take a look your existing uses of `<strong>`. If you were expressing strong emphasis as defined in HTML4, go ahead and make the changes noted above to nested `<em>` elements. If you intended some other semantic, use a plain `<span>` with a semantic class name.

The new `<strong>` element may also be nested to indicate increasing levels of importance.

SEMANTIC RECASTING OF HTML4 ELEMENTS

A small handful of presentational HTML4 elements have been recast with semantic meaning in HTML5.

<SMALL> DISCLAIMERS, CAVEATS, AND COPYRIGHTS

The `<small>` element is now used to express a set of semantics present on nearly every web page. Things such as

- small print legalese
- disclaimers
- caveats
- copyright statements

When you're updating pages, at a minimum wrap copyright statements in the new semantic `<small>` element.

<I>NSTANCES OF IDIOMS AND TAXONOMIC TERMS

The formerly presentational `<i>` (for italics) element has been redefined to semantically express the following:

- idioms
- terms from taxonomies (such as names of species)
- technical terms
- ship names

The new `<i>` element represents a set of disparate text semantics, all of which were typically styled with italics per common style guidelines.

<B>OLD LEADS, KEYWORDS, PRODUCTS, AND OTHER STYLISTIC OFFSETS

The `<b>` element has always meant bold, until now. Similar to the reverse semantic derivation of the new `<i>` element, the new `<b>` element now represents one or more of the following:

- keyword
- product name
- lead sentence or paragraph
- other text that is stylistically offset for some semantic reason

While at first this set of semantics seems arbitrary, these uses are similar and fairly frequent in practice. Stylistically offset text covers the more specific cases and illustrates why the new `<b>` makes sense semantically.

EAKING LINES FOR FUN AND POETRY

During the rediscovery of semantic HTML4 in the early 2000s, web designers found semantic uses for
 — in particular for lines in poetry and addresses. HTML5 has codified this practice.

With microformats, it turns out we no longer need <br> elements to express separation between the different components of an address.

In particular, with hCard and adr, we now mark up addresses as:

```
<div class="vcard">
    <div class="fn org">US Library of Congress</div>
    <div class="adr">
        <div class="street-address">101 Independence Ave. SE</div>
        <span class="locality">Washington</span>,
        <span class="region">DC</span>
        <span class="postal-code">20540-0002</span>
        <div class="country-name">United States of America</div>
    </div>
</div>
```

This expresses the address components, and indicates that the address belongs to an organization. Thus, poetry is the primary remaining semantic use for `<br>`.

HORIZONTAL RULES AND THEMATIC BREAKS

HTML5 reclaims the <hr> element to separate paragraphs at a thematic break.

Books often use ornate breaks and flourishes between paragraphs to indicate a meaningful shift in context, and that's exactly the semantic the new `<hr>` element is intended to convey.

HTML BLACK SHEEP ACKNOWLEDGED

Several elements and attributes, both in HTML4 and never before a part of any W3C specification, have been incorporated into HTML5.

THE iFRAME ELEMENT

The `<iframe>` element was long regarded as unnecessary; replaced with an `<object type="text/html">`. However, embedding one HTML document inside another remained useful, and HTML5 recognizes it `<iframe>`.

The new `seamless` attribute removes default presentation (borders, scrollbars) that browsers place around iframes.

```
<iframe src="embedded.html" seamless="seamless">
    Your browser doesn't support iframes, otherwise you would see embedded.html
</iframe>
```

THE EMBED ELEMENT

For years browsers have supported the embedding of plug-ins such as Flash and QuickTime via the `<embed>` element, yet it never made it into any W3C specification — until now.

HTML5 recognizes `<embed>` since a good portion of the web depends on it for interactive games, advertisements, streaming video, and the like.

```
<embed src="catgame.swf">
```

Numerous lengthy texts are written about how to use the `<embed>` element for specific plug-ins such as Flash and QuickTime, so I will not replicate that here.

THE TARGET ATTRIBUTE

HTML4 mistakenly deprecated the target attribute, presuming it to be presentational. Since HTML5 recognizes `<iframe>` it includes the target attribute as well.

- `<a target="t1">` - the hyperlink targets the iframe or window named "t1".
- `<area target="t1">` - the imagemap area link targets "t1".
- `<base target="t1">` - all links target "t1" by default.

LISTS: EMPTY, NUMBERED, AND REVERSED

HTML4 forbade empty lists; both `<ol>` and `<ul>` elements were required to have at least one `<li>` inside. Today's web applications can create empty lists that are later filled in with scripts, thus HTML5 permits them.

Two list numbering attributes were mistakenly deprecated in HTML4. HTML5 acknowledges that numbering both specific items and whole ordered lists communicates underlying semantics.

Use the value attribute on a list item to give it a particular number:

```
<!DOCTYPE html>
<meta charset="utf-8">
<title>League Results</title>

<ol>
    <li value="1">Peter</li>
    <li value="2">tied - Hana</li>
    <li value="2">tied - Gabriel</li>
    <li value="4">Molly</li>
    <li>Charlie</li>
</ol>
```

Results list with a tie for second.

For lists that start at a certain number, use the start attribute:

```
<!DOCTYPE html>
<meta charset="utf-8">
<title>League Results p.2</title>

<ol start="6">
    <li>Monica</li>
    <li>Kaito</li>
    <li>Eden</li>
    <li>Micah</li>
    <li>Angela</li>
</ol>
```

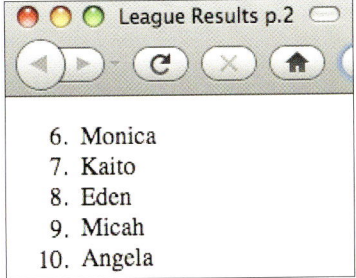

The second page of an ordered list that uses the start attribute to continue the numbering.

When using the `start` attribute, the entire list is numbered automatically, and there is no need to explicitly number each individual list item.

Lastly, HTML5 adds the `reversed` attribute to count down rather than up.

07
HTML5 FLEXIBILITY, UNIVERSALITY, AND CONSISTENCY

In this chapter we cover the last of the major changes from HTML4 to HTML5 — all of which make HTML easier to learn and use.

FLEXIBILITY: HYPERLINKS AND BLOCKS

HTML4 forbade you from linking entire headings, paragraphs, blockquotes, etc. HTML5 now lets you do so, because browsers have supported it for years. Bloggers typically link their post headlines to their permalinks and put the hyperlinks inside the headings to make them validate.

```
<h3>
    <a rel="bookmark" href="http://example.com/blog/3">Less is more</a>
</h3>
```

With HTML5, you have the flexibility of wrapping links around headings:

```
<a rel="bookmark" href="http://example.com/blog/3">
    <h3>Less is more</h3>
</a>
```

UNIVERSALITY: GLOBAL ATTRIBUTES

HTML5 finally allows the following attributes on all elements: `class`, `dir`, `id`, `lang`, `style`, `tabindex`, `title`.

These attributes always *seemed* global — but weren't until now.

The new global `class` attribute in particular enables you to mark up an entire page as being a specific microformat, such as an hCard:

```
<!DOCTYPE html>
<html class="vcard">
<meta charset="utf-8">
<title class="fn">Tantek Çelik</title>
<p>
    Hi, I'm Tantek and this is my simple home page at
    <a class="url" href="http://tantek.com/">tantek.com</a>.
    You can also find me on Twitter as
    <a rel="me" class="url" href="http://twitter.com/t">@t</a>
<p>
</html>
```

Or any other microformat that represents the entire page. See microformats.org for a list of microformats.

CONSISTENCY: MEDIA, HREFLANG, REL FOR ALL LINKS

HTML4 introduced the ability to specify which types of media that `<link>` elements applied to — for example, you could indicate a print style sheet:

```
<link media="print" rel="stylesheet" href="default.css">
```

HTML5 adds the `media` attribute to the `<a>` and `<area>` elements.

Press sites can semantically link to alternate print versions of articles.

```
<a media="print" rel="alternate" href="article-print.html">
    print version
</a>
```

Many sites have separate mobile sites that they can now link to semantically:

```
<a media="handheld" rel="alternate" href="http://m.example.com/">
    mobile site
</a>
```

HTML5 also fixes the <area> element. You may now use the following attributes on all <a>, <area>, and <link> elements:

- `media` (to indicate applicable media)
- `hreflang` (language of the destination)
- `rel` (relation of the destination to the source)

08
ADOPTED FROM XHTML 1.1: RUBY

Only one major new feature has survived from the otherwise evolutionary dead-end of XHTML 1.1 The `<ruby>` element — along with its children, `<rt>` and `<rp>` — are for marking up short bits of text with "ruby" annotations, used in East Asian typography for pronunciation or other annotations.

The `<rt>` element is for marking up the **r**uby **t**ext annotations themselves, and `<rp>` is used to mark up the **r**uby **p**arentheses that separate the annotation from the text they are annotating.

```
. . .
<ruby>
漢 <rp>(</rp><rt>かん</rt><rp>)</rp>
字 <rp>(</rp><rt>じ</rt><rp>)</rp>
</ruby>
. . .
```

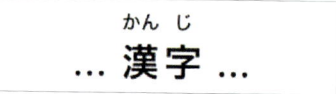

The two main ideographs, each with its annotation in hiragana rendered in a smaller font above it.

Browsers that support the <ruby> element place the ruby text near but offset from the ruby base and do not display the parentheses that separate the ruby text, hiding all the <rp> elements and their contents. Include <rp> elements and parentheses for fallback rendering in browsers that don't support <ruby>.

```
. . .
<ruby>
漢 <rp>(</rp><rt>かん</rt><rp>)</rp>
字 <rp>(</rp><rt>じ</rt><rp>)</rp>
</ruby>
. . .
```

... 漢 (かん) 字 (じ) ...

The two main ideographs, each with its annotation in hiragana rendered inside parentheses immediately following each respective ideograph.

09
CHECKPOINT: VALIDATING HTML5

The W3C Validator at http://validator.w3.org has long been an indispensable tool for modern web designers and developers alike. The W3C Validator has been updated to validate HTML5 documents automatically by detecting the HTML5 `<!DOCTYPE html>`.

In addition to the W3C Validator, a new validator dedicated to checking HTML5, called Validator.nu, has a few more options for custom validating your HTML5 documents.

I recommend that you continue to use the W3C Validator as part of your web authoring workflow. When your documents validate there, go ahead and check them with Validator.nu as well.

10
NEW HTML5 SEMANTICS

HTML5 is finally upgrading the HTML4 tags with semantics commonly used across the web.

STANDARDIZED PAGE STRUCTURE

Common page-level structures consist of multiple sections: a header section, navigation (usually), a main content area, and a footer section. HTML5 provides the corresponding elements.

```
<DOCTYPE html><meta charset="utf-8">
<title>HTML5 structural elements</title>
<body>
   <section>
     <header>
       <nav>
       ...
       </nav>
     </header>
     <div>
       ...
     </div>
     <footer>
       ...
     </footer>
   </section>
</body>
```

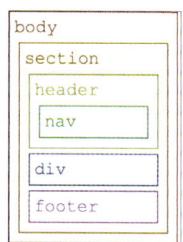

This outline demonstrates new HTML5 structural elements.

Strictly speaking, the top-level <section> element is unnecessary in the previous document, as the <body> element is enhanced by HTML5 to also be a "sectioning" element. A sectioning element sets a scope for various elements such as headings <h1> thru <h6> and the <address> element.

However, it is still good practice to use such a top-level section as it enhances the portability of your markup by turning your page into a building block. Sections can be nested to express the overall structure of more complex pages.

The new <header> element is for introductory material, navigation, and headings. If your section has navigation links you can simply wrap them in the new <nav> element.

There is no new "main" or "content" element that goes between the new <header> and <footer> elements. Use a plain old <div> for that purpose.

This brings us to the new `<footer>` element for information about the section such as authorship and copyright notices along with additional navigation links. Wherever you include clusters of navigation links, including inside a footer, wrap them in a `<nav>` element.

ARTICLES OF INDEPENDENCE

In addition to the hierarchy of sections with headers and footers, many web pages are themselves self-contained posts, entries, news items, or comments.

HTML5 introduces the `<article>` element, a special type of `<section>` element, to represent potentially independent content components that may be distributed or syndicated as items in feeds. `<article>` elements may be nested, e.g., a blog post would be an `<article>`, with comments on the post represented by nested `<article>` elements:

```
<article>
    I think HTML5 is pretty neat! -Tantek
    <article>
      But how useful is it really? -anonymous
    </article>
    <article>
      Use HTML5 for new semantics,
      native multimedia, and vector graphics. -Tantek
    </article>
</article>
```

TANGENTIAL ASIDES

Often, articles contain a few paragraphs of related material that didn't quite fit or flow in the main text (such as a sidebar to a magazine story). To represent such tangential topics, HTML5 introduces the new `<aside>` element.

```
<aside>
    <h1>After HTML5?</h1>
    <p>What happens <em>after</em> HTML5?
      Will there be an HTML6?
    </p>
</aside>
```

The `<aside>` element is also a special type of `<section>` element and thus can include its own headings and header and footer sections.

HEADING GROUPS: TWO AT A TIME OR PERHAPS MORE

In print, headings of various levels are often clustered together for greater effect.

Part of the cover of Neal Stephenson's book, *Diamond Age*, showing the title heading and subhead.

The full name of the book is split into a heading and a subhead with obvious stylistic differences. In HTML5, you can now semantically indicate such pairings (or more) of headings using the new `<hgroup>` element:

```
<hgroup>
    <h1>The Diamond Age</h1>
    <h2>or, A Young Lady's Illustrated Primer</h2>
</hgroup>
```

FIGURES, MARKS, AND DATES

The last set of new HTML5 semantic elements are the `<figure>`, `<mark>`, and `<time>` elements.

PICTURES ARE WORTH A FEW ASSOCIATED WORDS

Web authors have expressed the association between images and their captions for years.

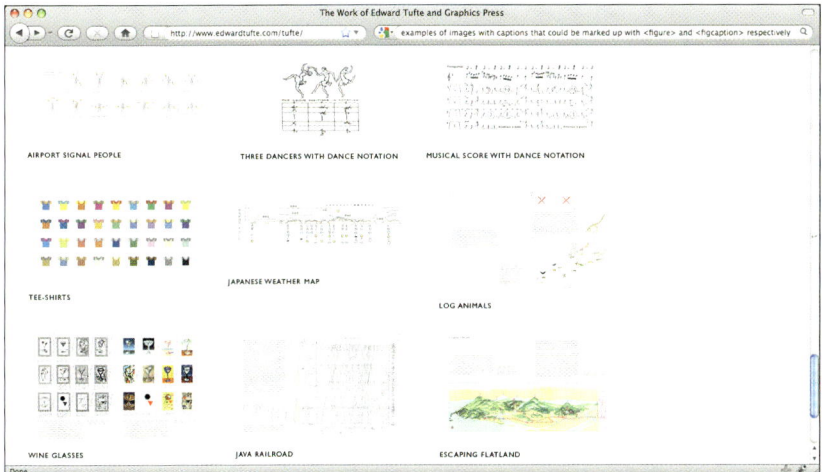

Part of Edward Tufte's home page showing a series of figures with associated captions.

HTML5 introduces the `<figure>` and `<figcaption>` elements to explicitly connect images with their captions.

```
<figure>
   <img src="figure1.png" alt="abstract figure example">
   <figcaption>Figure 1</figcaption>
</figure>
```

MARKED TEXT

HTML5 introduces the `<mark>` element to represent text that is highlighted for some reason outside its current context or by someone other than the author.

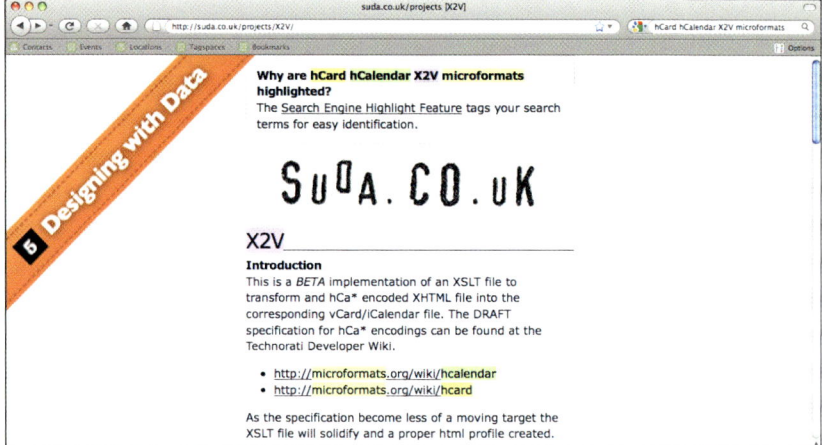

Brian Suda's X2V project page with highlight on the search terms used to find the page.

The highlights might be marked up with the <mark> element:

```
<p>Why are
    <mark class="t1">hCard</mark>
    <mark class="t2">hCalendar</mark>
    <mark class="t3">X2V</mark>
    <mark class="t4">microformats</mark>
    highlighted?
</p>
```

DATES AND TIMES

The new <time> element can be used to mark up either 24-hour time, a date, or date and time (with optional time zone).

```
<p>
    When I said <time>13:37</time>,
    I meant on <time>2010-03-03</time>,
    as in <time>2010-03-03T13:37</time>,
```

```
in particular <time>2010-03-03T13:37-0800</time>.
</p>
```

The first two uses of the `<time>` element are quite readable and understandable because more people worldwide understand 24-hour time and ISO dates than any other single (and often culture-specific) date or time format. The latter two examples use the ISO8601 datetime format and are not very human friendly.

The `<time>` element has a `datetime` attribute to specify a machine readable ISO8601 datetime, while placing a more human-friendly equivalent in the contents of the element:

```
<p>
    When I said <time>13:37</time>,
    I meant on <time>2010-03-03</time>,
    as in <time datetime="2010-03-03T13:37">1:37pm on March 3rd,
2010</time>,
    in particular <time datetime="2010-03-03T13:37-0800">1:37pm
PST</time>.
</p>
```

11
HTML5 NATIVE VECTOR GRAPHICS

HTML5 takes a major step forward with vector graphics support by incorporating two approaches:

- Inline SVG: the ability to place SVG markup directly into your HTML
- The `<canvas>` element: a graphics API for JavaScript

INLINE SVG

HTML5 defines how to natively embed and parse `<svg>` elements and their children. For example:

```
<p>
The following SVG should show a green circle:
    <svg>
      <circle r="50" cx="50" cy="50" fill="green"/>
    </svg>
</p>
```

No shipping browser supports this, but Firefox 4 and IE9 are expected to.

CANVAS

HTML5 introduces the new `<canvas>` element for drawing arbitrary vector graphics using JavaScript code in contrast to SVG's approach of using XML.

A simple canvas example shows two overlapping squares.

```
<!DOCTYPE html><meta charset="utf-8">
<title>Canvas example</title>
<script>
function draw()
{
```

```
    var canvas = document.getElementById("c1");
    if (canvas.getContext) {
        var c = canvas.getContext("2d");

        c.fillStyle = "rgb(171,213,16)";
        c.fillRect(32, 32, 96, 96);

        c.fillStyle = "rgba(255,0,102,0.75)";
        c.fillRect(64, 64, 96, 96);
    }
}
</script>
<body onload="draw();">
    <canvas id="c1" width="128" height="128">
      two overlapping squares.
    </canvas>
</body>
```

One of the best ways to learn is the time-honored web development practice of:

1. View source
2. Copy/paste
3. Make some changes
4. See what happened
5. Repeat steps 3–4 as necessary to understand how the code works

Let's copy/paste the `fillStyle`/`fillRect` lines of code to create another square of a different color:

```
    c.fillStyle = "rgba(255,0,102,0.75)";
    c.fillRect(64, 64, 96, 96);

    c.fillStyle = "rgba(0,0,255,0.5)";
    c.fillRect(96, 96, 96, 96);
```

The new code we added sets the `fillStyle` to a 50% transparent blue, and then draws another square 32 pixels down and to the right of the second square.

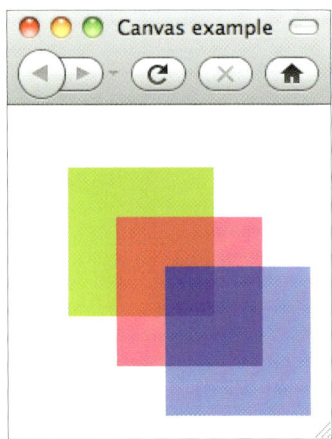

A simple canvas example now with three overlapping squares.

But we're not quite finished. One more bit to update remains: the fallback text.

```
<canvas id="c1" width="128" height="128">
    three overlapping squares.
</canvas>
```

Our complete updated example:

```
<!DOCTYPE html><meta charset="utf-8">
<title>Canvas example</title>
<script>
function draw()
{
    var canvas = document.getElementById("c1");
    if (canvas.getContext) {
      var c = canvas.getContext("2d");

      c.fillStyle = "rgb(171,213,16)";
      c.fillRect(32, 32, 96, 96);
```

```
    c.fillStyle = "rgba(255,0,102,0.75)";
    c.fillRect(64, 64, 96, 96);

    c.fillStyle = "rgba(0,0,255,0.5)";
    c.fillRect(96, 96, 96, 96);
    }
}
</script>
<body onload="draw();">
    <canvas id="c1" width="128" height="128">
      three overlapping squares.
    </canvas>
</body>
```

Numerous JavaScript drawing commands exist for the `<canvas>` element to perform all the usual graphics primitives. To learn more, see the Mozilla Developer Center online canvas tutorial: https://developer.mozilla.org/en/Canvas_tutorial.

12
HTML5 NATIVE AUDIO AND VIDEO

HTML5 introduces the `<audio>` and `<video>` elements, bringing rich declarative sound and motion to our otherwise static text and graphics.

AUDIO AND VIDEO BASICS

In their simplest forms, both new tags work like the trusty `<img>` tag, with a `src` attribute for the URL of the audio or video file respectively — except that both new tags have end tags as well.

```
<audio src="chess.wav"></audio>
<video src="chess.avi"></video>
```

SUPPORTING MULTIPLE FORMATS

The biggest challenge facing both `<audio>` and `<video>` elements is that there is currently no single format (either audio or video) that is natively supported across all browsers.

To demonstrate this, we're going to code another example, this time using some freely available open source/community video from the Internet Archive (archive.org). To get started, download the following video files:

- http://www.archive.org/download/Ryanne-BarCampSF816/Ryanne-BarCampSF816.ogv
- http://www.archive.org/download/Ryanne-BarCampSF816/Ryanne-BarCampSF816_512kb.mp4

Rename your local copies to just `barcampsf.ogv` and `barcampsf.mp4`.

Audio and video examples are nearly identical. In the remaining examples, we're going to focus on video — although they all apply to audio with just a change in formats.

A simple video example using the above files:

```
<!DOCTYPE html><meta charset="utf-8">
<title>video example</title>
<video src="barcampsf.mp4">
    A video showing BarCampSanFrancisco.
</video>
```

By default no controls are shown for video or audio. You can build your own controls from HTML elements styled with CSS, wired up to your audio and video elements with JavaScript. The full DOM APIs for controlling the `<audio>` and `<video>` elements are listed in the HTML5 specification itself. We're going to use the `controls` attribute to instruct the browser to give us a default set of `controls` so that we can focus on the content itself.

```
<video src="barcampsf.mp4" controls>
A video showing BarCampSanFrancisco.
</video>
```

If you post this example to your web site along with the video file, you can then view it using Safari, Chrome, or an iPad, as all of them use WebKit, which supports HTML5 video and also supports the H.264 format. Here is how Safari displays default video controls:

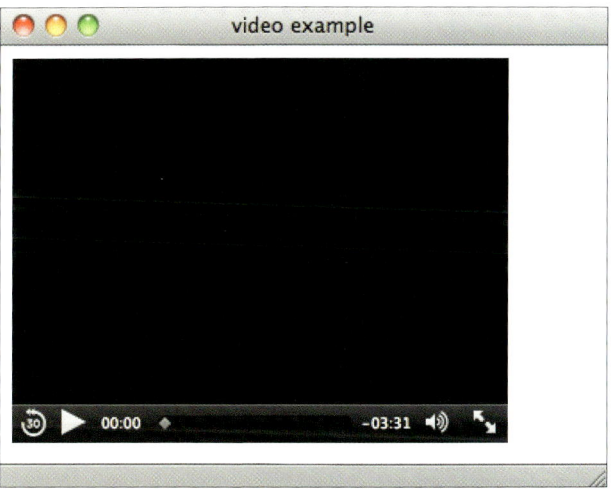

Firefox does not support the H.264 video format:

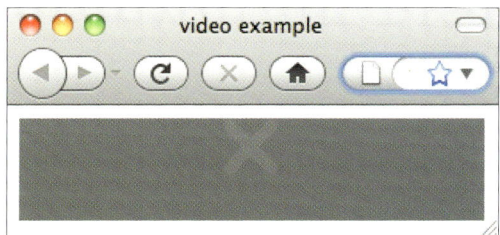

However, Firefox does support the Ogg Theora video format, and thus if we change the example to use Ogg instead of H.264:

```
<video src="barcampsf.ogv" controls>
    A video showing BarCampSanFrancisco.
</video>
```

Now it looks much better in Firefox:

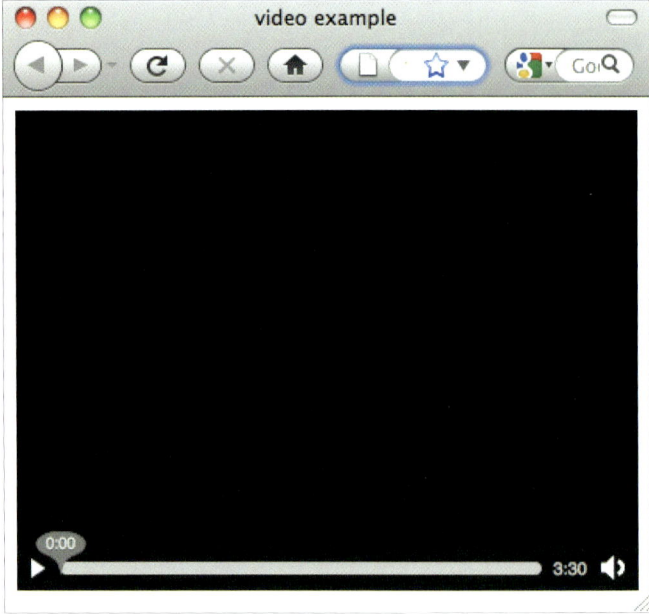

Expect different browsers — or even different devices with the same browser, such as desktop Safari vs. the iPad — to all have different default controls.

With the .ogv file, however, the video example doesn't work in Safari.

Safari handles failure worse than Firefox. Safari provides a play button and a "Loading…" status indicator, and indicates that if we just wait, the video will load and play, which is, of course, not true — Safari does not support Ogg Theora.

The challenge is to create an HTML5 video element that works in both.

HTML5 introduces a `<source>` element with an `src` attribute just like the `<audio>` and `<video>` elements themselves. Put `<source>` elements inside `<audio>` and `<video>` elements, in the order in which you want the browser to check their compatibility, followed by the fallback content for browsers that don't support the `<video>` element .

```
<video controls>
    <source src="barcampsf.ogv">
    <source src="barcampsf.mp4">
    A video showing BarCampSanFrancisco.
</video>
```

This example now works in both Safari and Firefox. For interactive demonstrations of the `<video>` element in various browsers, please see the HTML5 Now video.

13
NEW HTML5
USER INTERFACE ELEMENTS

When HTML was introduced in the early 1990s, the only semblance of interactivity it gave the user was the hyperlink — with a single click you could leap to any other page on the fledgling web.

In 1995, HTML 2.0 introduced forms and enabled e-commerce, adding profit-motive fuel to the fire of self-expression, and incredibly accelerating the growth of the web. A small number of user interface elements served as the building blocks for web applications, and a platform was born.

NEW FORM INPUTS

HTML5 adds more new `<input>` elements than all previous versions.

SEARCH

The new search input type is a special kind of text input that conveys the additional semantic that the user will be entering search terms.

```
<input type="search">
```

Browsers that understand this additional semantic can display the search input in a manner consistent with platform search interfaces.

Non-supporting browsers treat it like a normal text input. You can start using `<input type="search">` on your sites today.

TEL, URL, EMAIL

The new input types of tel, url, and email also represent special text inputs:

```
<input type="tel">
<input type="url">
<input type="email">
```

Browsers can present custom interfaces for entering phone numbers, web addresses, and email addresses. Mobile browsers on touch devices can present keyboards customized for frequently used keys, numbers and hyphens for phone numbers, slashes (/), dots (.), .com for URLs, @ for email addresses, etc. The iPhone offers such support.

NUMBER

Many web forms ask users to input numbers. The `<input type="number">` allows the browser to provide a custom interface for entering numbers.

COLOR

Many sites, such as Twitter, allow you to choose various colors for your profile page, including background, text, hyperlink, and other colors. For this purpose HTML5 introduces the color input:

`<input type="color">`

As of this writing, no browsers are known to support the color input.

DATE AND TIME INPUTS

In stark contrast to the limitations of the `<time>` element, there are numerous date and time inputs for specifying the date and time (with or without each other, local or not), a month, or a week.

```
<input type="date">
<input type="time">
<input type="datetime">
<input type="datetime-local">
<input type="month">
<input type="week">
```

BROWSER CHALLENGES

Opera 10.53 (the latest as of this writing) has problems sizing the inputs wide enough to display their values without clipping, and with the up/down arrow indicators on the right edges of most of the date and time inputs:

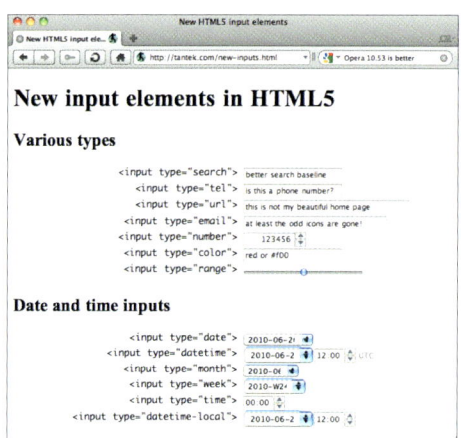

Other browsers have taken a more cautious approach, rendering very little (if anything) differently for the new input types. Version 5 of Safari has started to provide a hint of customization with little up/down buttons next to some of the new input types:

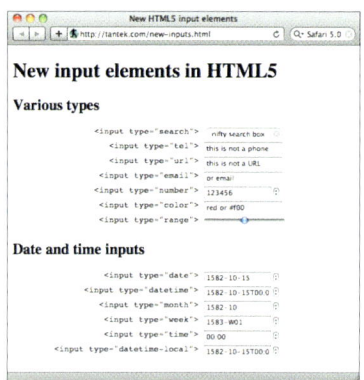

THE AUTOFOCUS, REQUIRED, AND PLACEHOLDER ATTRIBUTES

HTML5 adds more features for all input types, old and new alike. The first is the new autofocus attribute. On an `<input>` element, this attribute indicates to the browser that this input should be focused upon loading the page, so the user can start typing without having to first activate that input.

```
<input type="text" autofocus>
```

Many web forms have fields that users are required to fill in. Required fields often are indicated by an asterisk, a red border, or some other form of styling. HTML5 introduces the required attribute to make this semantic explicit:

```
<input type="text" required>
```

When browsers support the required attribute, they automatically alert users when they fail to complete one or more of the required fields in a form.

When creating forms, it can be quite useful to suggest to users what kind of information you're expecting in a specific field, and it may even make your user interface friendlier.

HTML5 introduces the placeholder attribute for providing such hints in form fields:

```
<input type="text" name="locality" placeholder="San Francisco">
<input type="text" name="region"  placeholder="California">
```

Webkit browsers (such as Safari and Chrome) and Opera support these new attributes, and Firefox will be supporting them soon. Start using them immediately, but be sure to still write your JavaScript with the expectation that not all browsers may support them.

OUTPUT AND DETAILS ELEMENTS

Many programs perform some sort of computation or calculation based on input from the user. For this purpose, HTML5 provides the `<output>` element. Obvious examples are calculators, financial projection applications, and other sites that take a bunch of numbers and provide some sort of result.

The `<details>` element is for representing and presenting a piece of content that offers a summary label with further details provided through a progressive disclosure interface. The new `<summary>` element marks up the summary or label inside the `<details>` element.

```
<details>
    <summary>shopping list</summary>
    <ul>
      <li>red wine</li>
      <li>dark chocolate</li>
    </ul>
</details>
```

No current browsers support the interactivity portion of the `<details>` element. These new elements have been among the more unstable in the HTML5 specification.

METER, RANGE, AND PROGRESS

HTML5 introduces a few elements for displaying and inputting ranges of values. The new `<meter>` element can be used to display measurements such as a score, a rating, a countdown, or donations towards a goal. The new element comes with `min` and `max` attributes to set the bottom and top ends of the range, as well as a `value` attribute.

```
<meter value="74" max="100"> 74% </meter>
<meter value="0.75"> 3/4 </meter>
```

On the input side, there is also an input type for entering a measurement along a range of values, `<input type="range">`, also with `min`, `max`, and `value` attributes:

```
<input type="range" min="0" max="100" value="74">
```

For the special case of progress towards completion of a task, HTML5 introduces the `<progress>` element. This element also has `max` and `value` attributes, but has a fixed minimum of zero (0):

```
<progress value="75" max="100"> 75% complete </progress>
```

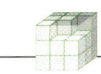

The `<progress>` element can also indicate indeterminate progress when there is no estimate available. Use the `<progress>` element on your sites to indicate how far along various user tasks are, such as uploading, online checkout, or multipage forms. To indicate indeterminate progress, omit the `value` attribute:

```
<progress> working... </progress>
```

For both the `<meter>` and `<progress>` elements, always include fallback text. Although browser support for the `<meter>`, `<input type="range">`, and `<progress>` elements is currently quite sparse, recent improvements in particular in Safari show promise:

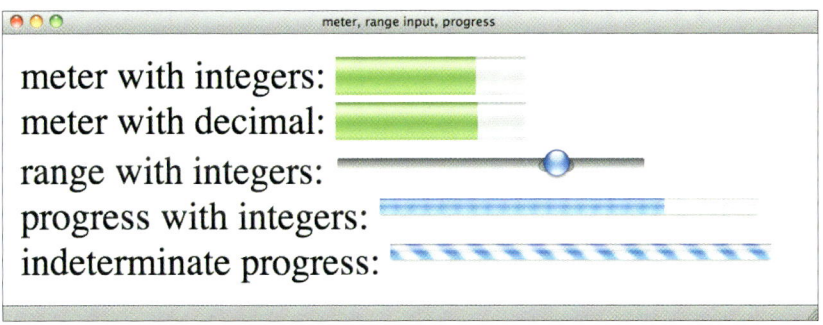

A common theme throughout all these new HTML5 user interface elements is the variance in levels of implementation across browsers, which change rapidly with each release. It's both exciting to see, and challenging to design for.

14
THE HTML5 BLEEDING EDGE

With all the immediate practical utility that HTML5 brings, a larger concept of HTML5 is broadly championed and cheered on by web developers worldwide and promoted by companies as large as Apple and Google.

As marketed, the concept would be more accurately framed as "The Open Web Applications Platform," and includes both well established technologies like microformats, CSS, and unobtrusive JavaScript and a set of working drafts, some of which were spun off from HTML5 and others of which were never part of HTML5.

Geolocation API (http://www.w3.org/TR/geolocation-API). Allows a web page to ask the browser for geolocation information about where the user is.

HTML Device (http://dev.w3.org/html5/html-device). For accessing various hardware capabilities, such as built-in cameras or microphones.

Microdata (http://www.w3.org/TR/microdata). A way to annotate content in HTML with custom vocabularies, in many ways much simpler than RDFa. Use microformats that are already well supported first and take a look at microdata if you want to create your own vocabulary.

Web Sockets API (http://www.w3.org/html5/websockets). Defines an API for two-way communication between web pages and servers.

Web SQL Database (http://www.w3.org/TR/webdatabase). Defines an API for storing data in a database in the web browser and querying it with a variant of SQL.

Indexed Database API (http://www.w3.org/TR/IndexedDB) defines a database of hierarchical object records with key/value pairs.

Web Storage (http://www.w3.org/TR/webstorage). Stores key/value pairs.

Web Workers (http://www.w3.org/TR/workers). An API for creating additional background JavaScript threads.

Web Messaging (http://dev.w3.org/html5/postmsg). Defines mechanisms for communicating between different browser windows, tabs, and iframes.

All these "specifications" are W3C public working drafts or editor's drafts, which means that they all issue the following warning about their status (emphasis from source): "Implementors should be aware that this specification is not stable. **Implementors who are not taking part in the discussions are likely to find the specification changing out from under them in incompatible ways."**

15
CHECKPOINT: REVALIDATE

By now you've added at least a few new HTML5 features to your pages. Time to revalidate your pages.

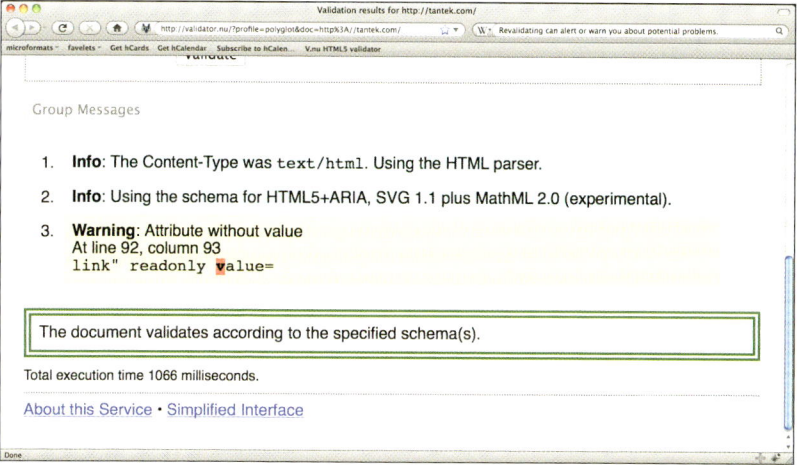

Even if your document validates, pay close attention to any warnings and see if there is something you can improve. In this case, the validator is warning that I have an "Attribute without value."

In Chapter 5, I noted that all attribute values must be quoted for XHTML compatibility. When checking my documents for both HTML and XHTML validity, the validator noted a particular case of an unquoted value: not having an explicit value at all!

HTML has several such "standalone" attributes. New XHTML compatibility requires that they have explicitly quoted values. Use the name of the attribute as a value for itself:

```
<input type="url" id="link" readonly="readonly" value="..." />
```

Applying that fix, let's take a look at what Validator.nu reports:

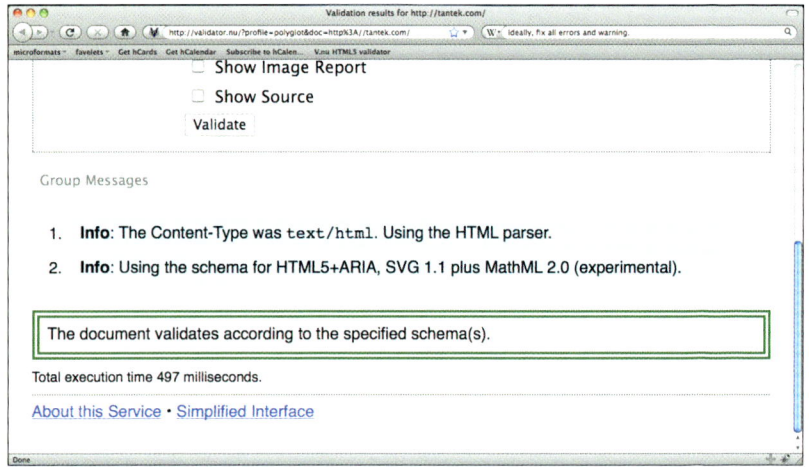

Repeat this process of validating, finding the sources of errors or warnings, fixing them, and revalidating until you have fixed all errors/warnings and the validator returns a clean green validation report.

Congratulations! You're now using HTML5.

16
CONCLUSION

We've covered a lot about HTML5, and no doubt you will have further questions, want to both keep up with the spec as it evolves, and perhaps even help it do so.

KEEPING UP WITH HTML5 EVOLUTION

You now have a good idea of what HTML5 currently does and doesn't do. I recommend following updates to the these resources for keeping up with changes.

The HTML5 Now Twitter (http://twitter.com/html5now [@html5now])

The HTML5 Now Wiki (http://html5now.pbwiki.com)

HTML5 differences from HTML4 (http://w3.org/TR/html5-diff)

HTML: The Markup Language (http://w3.org/TR/html-markup)

MORE HTML5 RESOURCES

There are a few good HTML5 books that have been recently released or soon will be that will help provide additional depth and perspective on HTML5.

HTML5 for Web Designers by Jeremy Keith

HTML5: Up and Running by Mark Pilgrim

Introducing HTML5 by Bruce Lawson and Remy Sharp

For additional perspectives on HTML5, I recommend the following blogs:

WHATWG blog (http://blog.whatwg.org)

Ian Hickson (http://ln.hixie.ch)

Jeremy Keith (http://adactio.com/journal/tag/html5)

Bruce Lawson (http://www.brucelawson.co.uk/category/html5)

Jeffrey Zeldman (http://www.zeldman.com/category/html5)

HELP IMPROVE HTML5 WHILE LEARNING

HTML5 is still a working draft, and needs your feedback, input, and suggestions. Here are some resources to participate in the evolution of HTML5:

WHATWG wiki: (http://wiki.whatwg.org) A very good resource for tracking and contributing research and proposals for changes to HTML5.

#whatwg IRC channel on Freenode IRC (irc://irc.freenode.org/whatwg): A lot of informal communication takes place on the IRC channel, and HTML5 experts are there nearly every hour of the day. This is a good place to start if you think you've found a problem in HTML5 and/or have suggestions for improvement.

W3C HTML Working Group (http://www.w3.org/html/wg/#join): The HTML Working Group is open for anyone to join. All you need to do is fill out a few forms, agree to share your contributions freely (e.g. that you're not going to assert any patents), and you can join the HTML Working Group mailing list and participate directly in HTML5 discussions at W3C.

HTML5 NOW

You've learned everything you need to know to write your first HTML5 document, update your HTML4/XHTML1 documents to HTML5, enhance your pages with new semantics, graphics, and multimedia support, validate and fix your pages as necessary, and publish your HTML5 site!

Thank you for reading this book and watching the video. You can make a difference in your pages, on the web, and for the web. I look forward to seeing your work.

Tantek Çelik, http://tantek.com
San Francisco, California, U.S.A.